Discipleship

JOHN A. STEWART

Lamplighters International is a Christian ministry that helps individuals engage with God and His Word and equips believers to be disciple-makers.

For additional information about Lamplighters ministry resources, contact:

Lamplighters International
771 NE Harding Street, Suite 250
Minneapolis, MN USA 55413
or visit our website at
www.LamplightersUSA.org

Product Code DM-NK-2P

ISBN 978-1-931372-46-6

First Printing, June 2019

CONTENTS

How to Use This Study

What Is Lamplighters?

Lamplighters is a Christian ministry that helps individuals engage with God and His Word and equips believers to be disciple-makers. This Bible study, comprising six individual lessons, is a self-contained unit and an integral part of the entire discipleship ministry. When you have completed the study, you will have a much greater understanding of a portion of God's Word, with many new truths that you can apply to your life.

How to study a Lamplighters Lesson

A Lamplighters study begins with prayer, your Bible, the weekly lesson, and a sincere desire to learn more about God's Word. The questions are presented in a progressive sequence as you work through the study material. You should not use Bible commentaries or other reference books (except a dictionary) until you have completed your weekly lesson and met with your weekly group. Approaching the Bible study in this way allows you to personally encounter many valuable spiritual truths from the Word of God.

To gain the most out of the Bible study, find a quiet place to complete your weekly lesson. Each lesson will take approximately 45–60 minutes to complete. You will likely spend more time on the first few lessons until you are familiar with the format, and our prayer is that each week will bring the discovery of important life principles.

The writing space within the weekly studies provides the opportunity for you to answer questions and respond to what you have learned. Putting answers in your own words, and including Scripture references where appropriate, will help you personalize and commit to memory the truths you have learned. The answers to the questions will be found in the Scripture references at the end of each question or in the passages listed at the beginning of each lesson.

If you are part of a small group, it's a good idea to record the specific dates that you'll be meeting to do the individual lessons. Record the specific dates each time the group will be meeting next to the lesson titles on the Contents page. Additional lines have been provided for you to record when you go through this same study at a later date.

The side margins in the lessons can be used for the spiritual insights you glean from other group or class members. Recording these spiritual truths will likely be a spiritual help to you and others when you go through this study again in the future.

AUDIO INTRODUCTION

Audio introductions are available for all Lamplighters studies and are a great resource for the group leader. They can also be used to introduce the study to your group. To access the audio introductions, go to www.LamplightersUSA. org.

"DO YOU THINK?" QUESTIONS

Each weekly study has a few *"do you think?"* questions designed to help you to make personal applications from the biblical truths you are learning. In the first lesson the *"do you think?"* questions are placed in italic print for easy identification. If you are part of a study group, your insightful answers to these questions could be a great source of spiritual encouragement to others.

PERSONAL QUESTIONS

Occasionally you'll be asked to respond to personal questions. If you are part of a study group you may choose not to share your answers to these questions with the others. However, be sure to answer them for your own benefit because they will help you compare your present level of spiritual maturity to the biblical principles presented in the lesson.

A FINAL WORD

Throughout this study the masculine pronouns are frequently used in the generic sense to avoid awkward sentence construction. When the pronouns *he*, *him*, and *his* are used in reference to the Trinity (God the Father, Jesus Christ, and the Holy Spirit), they always refer to the masculine gender.

This Lamplighters study was written after many hours of careful preparation. It is our prayer that it will help you "… grow in the grace and knowledge of our Lord and Savior Jesus Christ. To Him be the glory both now and forever. Amen" (2 Peter 3:18).

What Is an Intentional Discipleship Bible Study?
The *Next Step* in Bible Study

The Lamplighters Bible study series is ideal for individual, small group, and classroom use. This Bible study is also designed for Intentional Discipleship training. An Intentional Discipleship (ID) Bible study has four key components. Individually they are not unique, but together they form the powerful core of the ID Bible study process.

1. Objective: Lamplighters is a discipleship training ministry that has a dual objective: (1) to help individuals engage with God and His Word and (2) to equip believers to be disciple-makers. The small group format provides extensive opportunity for ministry training, and it's not limited by facilities, finances, or a lack of leadership staffing.

2. Content: The Bible is the focus rather than Christian books. Answers to the study questions are included within the study guides, so the theology is in the study material, not in the leader's mind. This accomplishes two key objectives: (1) It gives the group leader confidence to lead another individual or small group without fear, and (2) it protects the small group from theological error.

3. Process: The ID Bible study process begins with an Open House, which is followed by a 6–14-week study, which is followed by a presentation of the Final Exam (see graphic on page 8). This process provides a natural environment for continuous spiritual growth and leadership development.

4. Leadership Development: As group participants grow in Christ, they naturally invite others to the groups. The leader-trainer (1) identifies and recruits new potential leaders from within the group, (2) helps them register for online discipleship training, and (3) provides in-class leadership mentoring until they are both competent and confident to lead a group according to the ID Bible study process. This leadership development process is scalable, progressive, and comprehensive.

OVERVIEW OF THE LEADERSHIP TRAINING AND DEVELOPMENT PROCESS

There are three stages of leadership training in the Intentional Discipleship process: (1) leading studies, (2) training leaders, and (3) multiplying groups (see appendix for greater detail).

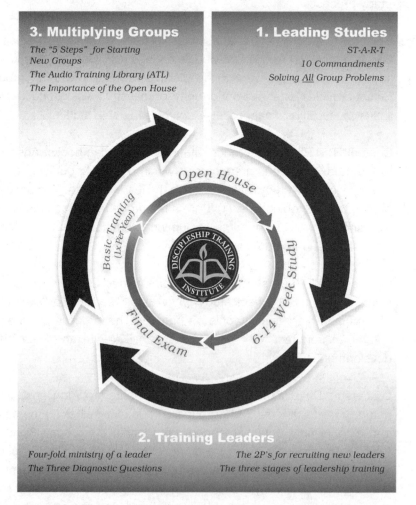

Intentional Discipleship
Training & Development Process

3. Multiplying Groups

The "5 Steps" for Starting New Groups
The Audio Training Library (ATL)
The Importance of the Open House

1. Leading Studies

ST-A-R-T
10 Commandments
Solving All Group Problems

Open House

Basic Training (1x Per Year)

6-14 Week Study

Final Exam

DISCIPLESHIP TRAINING INSTITUTE

2. Training Leaders

Four-fold ministry of a leader
The Three Diagnostic Questions

The 2P's for recruiting new leaders
The three stages of leadership training

How Can I Be Trained?

Included within this Bible study is the student workbook for Level 1 (Basic Training). Level 1 training is both free and optional. Level 1 training teaches you a simple 4-step process (ST-A-R-T) to help you prepare a life-changing Bible study and 10 proven small group leadership principles that will help your group thrive. To register for a Level 1 online training event, either as an individual or as a small group, go to www.LamplightersUSA.org/training or www.discipleUSA. org. If you have additional questions, you can also call 800-507-9516.

ONE

IS THERE A WORD FROM THE LORD?

Read Psalm 119:97–105; John 5:39; 2 Timothy 3:16–17; 2 Peter 1:16–21; other references as given.

Everyone needs purpose. A young boy may dream about becoming a firefighter or a star athlete and a young girl about being a princess, a famous singer, or a doctor. An adult may envision building great buildings or discovering a cure for a dreaded disease. Every person, child or adult, must have a purpose in life and seek to fulfill it. Without purpose, hope is lost, dreams crumble, and people die even though they are still alive.

The same is true for the believer. A believer must understand why God has saved him and accept his God-given identity in Christ. The Christian's purpose is to glorify God (1 Corinthians 6:19–20; 10:31) and make disciples of all nations (Matthew 28:18–20). The command to make disciples of Jesus Christ is known as the Great Commission.

Discipleship is God's call to believers to join Him to help all people submit to the Lord Jesus Christ in all things. God's call is *personal*. Every believer has been called to make disciples. God's call is *authoritative*. Jesus said, **"Go into all the world and preach the gospel"** (Mark 16:15). God's call is *effective*. His call to make disciples implies effective ministry through the power of the Holy Spirit. God's call is *comprehensive*. Jesus has all authority, and all believers are to make disciples of all nations and teach them **to observe all things** (Matthew 28:20). For the believer to not accept God's calling to make disciples is to miss his purpose and mission in life.

Lombardi Time Rule:

If the leader arrives early, he or she has time to pray, prepare the room, and greet others personally.

———

ADD GROUP INSIGHTS BELOW

In this first lesson you'll learn that discipleship doesn't begin with a method or even a message—God's command to make disciples and the believer's response to Jesus' call. It begins with Jesus Christ, who died on a cross to save man and now calls us to join Him in a great holy cause.

Before you begin, ask God to reveal Himself to you and transform you into the image of Jesus Christ.

1. God is a god who communicates. This is one of the most important truths for a Christian to learn. In Genesis 1:1, the Bible says, **In the beginning God ...** and His revelation to man continues throughout Scripture. The Bible is His-story and His revelation of Himself to man.

    a. What two-word response did Jeremiah give King Zedekiah when he was asked, **"Is there any word from the Lord?"**(Jeremiah 37:16–17)?

        _____

    b. If someone asked you if there is any word from the Lord, meaning do you believe the Bible is God's divinely inspired revelation to man, how would you answer this question?

        _____

        _____

        Why? _____

        _____

        _____

2. Religious liberals (religious nonbelievers) reject the belief that the Bible is the divinely inspired Word of God. They use nice-sounding statements like "The Bible contains the words of God, but it also includes the words of man" and "The Bible is inspired the way the masters of the past were inspired when they created great masterpieces of art, music, and literature." Most evangelicals (those who have been

born again through faith in Jesus Christ), however, believe the Bible is the divinely inspired, inerrant Word of God.

a. There are three possibilities about the precise nature of the Bible; (1) The Bible is the words of man, 2) The Bible contains the words of God and the words of man, and (3) The Bible is what it claims to be—God's inerrant revelation. Which of these three possibilities *do you think* describes the exact nature of the Bible?

_____

_____

Why? _____

_____

_____

b. What does the Bible claim about its own nature (2 Timothy 3:16; 2 Peter 1:20–21)?

_____

_____

_____

3. The early church leader Augustine (354–430) said "If you believe what you like in the Gospel and reject what you do not like, it is not the Gospel you believe, but yourself." How does the Bible refute the liberal interpreters' claim that it contains both the words of God and the words of man (John 10:35)?

_____

_____

_____

4. The Bible's claim to be divinely inspired by God doesn't prove that it is the Word of God. Merely claiming something is true does not make it true (this is known as "circular

Zip-It Rule:

Group members should agree to disagree, but should never be disagreable.

———

ADDITIONAL INSIGHTS

reasoning"). There are four facts, however, that lead honest evaluators to one undeniable conclusion—that the Bible is the inspired Word of God. What *do you think* are these four undeniable facts that lead unbiased evaluators to conclude the Bible must be the divinely inspired Word of God?

1. _____

_____

2. _____

_____

3. _____

_____

4. _____

_____

5. Two phrases, *verbal inspiration* and *plenary inspiration*, are often used to describe the specific nature of God's Word. *Verbal* inspiration means the words, not just the thoughts, were inspired by God in the original writings (called manuscripts) of the Bible. The word *plenary* means all the words of the Bible are God-breathed. The Bible doesn't just contain the words of God; it is the Word of God. Even though most evangelical Christians believe the Bible is the inspired Word of God, many still struggle to understand the implications of biblical inspiration.

a. What is the fourfold ministry of God's Word (2 Timothy 3:16)?

1. _____

2. _____

3. _____

4. _____

b. What will be the result if you (1) accept the Bible for what it is, the divinely inspired Word of God and (2) allow it to impact your life (2 Timothy 3:17)?

_____

_____

_____

Want to learn how to disciple another person, lead a life-changing Bible study or start another study? Go to www.Lamplighters USA.org/training to learn how.

ADDITIONAL
INSIGHTS

  c. If you are a Christian, *do you think* God's Word can thoroughly furnish or equip you to fulfill His command to make disciples of Jesus Christ?

      ❏ Yes   ❏ No   ❏ I am not sure.

      ❏ I never thought about that before.

6. What did Peter say about the sufficiency of God's Word (2 Peter 1:3)?

_____

_____

7. In which areas listed below *do you think* the Bible is trustworthy and should be accepted as completely true? Seriously consider each category before answering.

1. God	❏ YES	❏ NO
2. Origin of life	❏ YES	❏ NO
3. Man's nature	❏ YES	❏ NO
4. Marriage/sexuality	❏ YES	❏ NO
5. Science	❏ YES	❏ NO
6. Sin	❏ YES	❏ NO
7. Meaning of life	❏ YES	❏ NO
8. Peace/happiness	❏ YES	❏ NO
9. Finances	❏ YES	❏ NO
10. Eternal life	❏ YES	❏ NO

8. Because the Bible is true, His Word is authoritative, complete, comprehensive, and thoroughly adequate to equip you to do all He has commanded you.

  a. Jesus said, **"Go and make disciples of all nations"** (Matthew 28:19), but only a small number of Christians respond to His command in an intentional way. Why *do you think* many believers are not intentional about obeying Christ's command to make disciples?

_____

_____

_____

_____

b. If you are a believer, how are you actively fulfilling Christ's command to make disciples?

_____

_____

_____

_____

9. If you are a Christian, the Bible says that God has given you everything that pertains to life and godliness, including everything you need to make disciples. Are you willing, even if you don't know how, to obey God and make disciples of Jesus Christ?

_____

_____

10. What is the most important truth you learned from this lesson?

_____

_____

_____

_____

_____

_____

Two

Does God Have a Plan?

Read 1 Corinthians 3:9–15; Ephesians 1:7–10; Hebrews 11:8–16; other references as given.

Discipleship is God's call to believers to join Him to help all people submit to the Lord Jesus Christ in all things. If you are a Christian, God has called you to make disciples of Jesus Christ (Matthew 28:18–20; Mark 16:15; John 20:21; Acts 1:8). You don't need a special call or message from God to do what He has commanded you to do in His Word. God's call is also effective because He never commands believers to do anything without giving them the grace to accomplish His will (2 Peter 1:3–4).

In this lesson you'll learn the answer to two important questions: (1) "Does God have a master plan?" and (2) "If God has a master plan, how do I as a believer fit into His plan?" Only when a believer knows God's plan and understands how he fits into His plan can he embrace his calling and fulfill his mission in this life.

Before you begin, ask God to reveal Himself to you and to transform you into the image of Jesus Christ.

Volunteer Rule:

If the leader asks for volunteers to read, pray, and answer the questions, group members will be more inclined to invite newcomers.

ADD GROUP
INSIGHTS BELOW

1. People have various ideas about God and the presence of evil in this world. Some believe God doesn't exist and the events of life are merely the result of time and chance and the choices people make. Others believe God exists, but He is not all-powerful. According to this view, God and evil are engaged in a great cosmic battle with each claiming victory at certain times. Still others believe God is sovereign, but His

original plan was thwarted when Adam's sin caused God to go to "Plan B." List three reasons why Jesus came into this world.

1. Luke 19:10: _____

_____

_____

2. John 13:12–15; 1 Peter 2:21: _____

_____

_____

3. 1 John 3:8: _____

_____

_____

2. Many people are confused who God is and even more are confused about what He is doing in this world. The Bible, however, tells us who God is and what His master plan is for His creation. The New Living Translation (NLT) captures His plan in plain English when it says, **"This is the plan: At the right time he will bring everything together under the authority of Christ—everything in heaven and on earth"** (Ephesians 1:10). If you are a Christian, how do you think you fit into God's plan?

_____

_____

_____

3. The Bible uses several analogies or comparisons to teach believers about their relationship with God and other believers, as well as how God wants to employ them within His master plan. Each of the following analogies teaches a different aspect of the believer's ministry before the Lord. Identify the various roles of the believer and give a brief description of the corresponding responsibility.

	Role/designation	Responsibility
a. 1 Corinthians 3:5–9		
b. 1 Corinthians 3:10–14		
c. 1 Corinthians 12:12–26		
d. 1 Peter 2:9–10		
e. 1 Peter 2:11		

59:59 Rule:

Participants appreciate when the leader starts and finishes the studies on time—all in one hour (the 59:59 rule). If the leader doesn't complete the entire lesson, the participants will be less likely to do their weekly lessons and the Bible study discussion will tend to wander.

———

ADDITIONAL INSIGHTS

4. a. The Bible uses another powerful analogy to help believers understand their role and responsibility within God's master plan. What happens when an individual places his faith in Jesus Christ for salvation (Colossians 1:13)?

_____

_____

_____

b. What does an individual become when he is transferred into the kingdom of Jesus Christ (Philippians 3:20)?

_____

_____

c. What is the believer's responsibility as a citizen of heaven (2 Corinthians 5:18–20)?

_____

_____

_____

5. It is often life-changing when a Christian realizes he is a citizen of heaven and God's ambassador. The Christian's conduct and speech, too often reflective of the world's values, are transformed when he understands that he is God's official emissary. In what ways do you think an ambassador for Christ and an earthly foreign diplomat are similar?

1. _____

_____

2. _____

_____

3. _____

_____

4. _____

_____

6. The Bible says Christians have been transferred from the domain of darkness into the kingdom of God's dear Son (Colossians 1:13).

a. Hebrews 11 is known as the "Hall of Faith" because it contains the testimonies of several Old Testament believers who walked with God and lived by faith. How did these believers view themselves while they were on earth (Hebrews 11:13)?

_____

_____

_____

b. If you are a Christian, do you view your time on earth in the same way? _____

Why? _____

_____

_____

_____

c. List three eternal things that they believed were better than anything this world could provide them.
   1. Abraham wanted a better _____ (Hebrews 11:8–10).
   2. They wanted a better _____ or _____ (Hebrews 11:13–16).
   3. They wanted a better _____ (Hebrews 11:35).

d. If you are a Christian, do you seek eternal things (God and the things that matter for eternity) more than you do temporal things (earthly values and priorities, materialism) so you will be given a better resurrection?

❏ Yes   ❏ No   ❏ Not as much as I should.
❏ No, because I like the things that are passing away.
❏ Yes, but I still struggle with wanting earthly things.

7. Another important aspect of the believer's relationship to God and His master plan is priesthood. When God originally called the Jewish people out of slavery in Egypt (Exodus), He instructed them to build a tabernacle or portable worship center (Exodus 26:1) which was later replaced by a permanent temple in Jerusalem. Both the tabernacle and temple consisted of a large outer enclosure and an inner covered structure that included two rooms (Exodus 26:33 — the holy place, the Most Holy Place). These two inner rooms were separated by a heavy curtain or veil. The high priest entered the Most Holy Place once a year on the Day of Atonement to intercede for the people and make atonement

for their sins (Leviticus 16). No one else could enter the Most Holy Place. List three significant events that took place when Jesus died on the cross (Matthew 27:51–53)?

1. _____

2. _____

3. _____

8. The tearing of the veil between the holy place and the Most Holy Place revealed a transition from the Old Covenant (Law of Moses), with its earthly priests and limited access to God, to the New Covenant with a new priestly order and a new High Priest, Jesus Christ (Hebrews 8:7–13, 9:6–10, 16–28). The tearing of the veil also indicated that all believers were given direct access to God through Jesus Christ, and they serve as priest-believers (1 Peter 2:9–10). Many believers, however, still live like they are under the Old Covenant with its limited access to God and earthly intermediaries. In what ways do you think a Christian's service to God should change when he realizes that he is both a priest-believer and an ambassador for Christ?

_____

_____

_____

_____

_____

9. What is the most important truth you learned from this lesson?

_____

_____

_____

_____

THREE

GREAT COMMISSION OR GREAT CONFUSION?

Read Matthew 28:18–20; Mark 16:15, Luke 24:46–49; John 20:21; Acts 1:8; other references as given.

In the last lesson you learned that all believers are citizens of heaven and God's ambassadors. You also learned Christ's death on the cross ushered in the New Covenant which gives believers direct access to God through Jesus Christ. At salvation Christians die to their old life (Romans 6:8; 1 Corinthians 6:19), but they become God's ambassadors who represent Him, wise builders who build truth into others, and priest-believers who offer up spiritual sacrifices to God and proclaim the gospel to the world.

In this lesson you'll learn what the Bible teaches about the Great Commission. The Great Commission is the Christian's official draft notice, conscripting all believers into God's mighty spiritual army. If you are a Christian, your number has been called. No additional draft notices will be sent to you. Either you will report for duty, or you will be a conscientious objector who will give account of yourself to God.

The Great Commission is comprised of five references in the New Testament – one in each of the Gospels and one in the book of Acts. To be an effective ambassador for Christ, you must (1) understand what the Great Commission teaches, (2) learn how to make disciples according to the biblical plan, and (3) step out in faith and trust the Holy Spirit to empower you.

Now ask God to reveal Himself to you and to transform you into the image of Jesus Christ.

Focus Rule:

If the leader helps the group members focus on the Bible, they will gain confidence to study God's Word on their own.

———

ADD GROUP INSIGHTS BELOW

1. a. Before we look at what the Bible teaches about the Great Commission, an important question must be answered: "Why does man need to be reconciled to God?" What does the Bible teach about (natural, unsaved) man's condition before God?

     1. Isaiah 53:6: _____

        _____

     2. Romans 3:12: _____

        _____

     3. Romans 3:19: _____

        _____

     4. Ephesians 2:1, 12: _____

        _____

   b. What happens if someone has not been reconciled to God before he dies (Revelation 20:11–15)?

      _____

      _____

      _____

2. Some Christians believe Christ's command to make disciples was given only to the apostles. Others believe the fulfillment of the Great Commission is the sole responsibility of church leaders and those with the gift of evangelism. How do we know Christ's command to make disciples (the Great Commission) applies to all Christians?

   1. Matthew 28:19; Mark 16:15: _____

      _____

      _____

   2. Romans 1:14; Ephesians 6:20: _____

      _____

      _____

3. How did the early church understand their responsibility to fulfill the Great Commission (Acts 8:4)?

_____

_____

_____

Drawing Rule:

To learn how to draw everyone into the group discussion without calling on anyone, go to www.Lamplighters USA.org/training.

_____

ADDITIONAL INSIGHTS

4. a. Five references (Matthew 28:18–20; Mark 16:15; Luke 24:46–49; John 20:21; Acts1:8) comprise the Great Commission. According to Mark 16:15, Jesus commanded His followers to preach the gospel to all the world. What is the gospel (1 Corinthians 15:1–4)?

_____

_____

_____

b. The apostle Paul warned the Galatian churches about receiving another or false gospel (Galatians 1:6–9). Which of the following statements reflects an *improper* understanding of the true gospel of Jesus Christ? Answer "Yes" if you believe it reflects an improper understanding, "No" if you believe it doesn't.

1. I became a Christian when I prayed the "Sinner's Prayer." _____

2. I became a Christian when I was baptized and joined the church. _____

3. I become a Christian when I take Communion.

_____

4. I've always been a Christian. I was born into a Christian home and believe Jesus lived. _____

5. I became a Christian when I asked Jesus into my heart. _____

5. Jesus commanded His followers to **preach the gospel to every creature** (Mark 16:15). In another Great Commission reference, Jesus said **repentance and remission of sins**

should be *preached* in His (Jesus') **name to all nations** (Luke 24:47). Mark 16:15 presents the *communication* to be preached (the gospel). 1 Corinthians 15:1–4 presents the *content* of the gospel (Jesus' death, burial, resurrection). Luke 24:47 presents the *call* (repentance) of the gospel, as well as the *consequence* (remission or forgiveness of sins) for those who believe.

a. What did Paul tell the jailer when he asked, **"What must I do to be saved?"** (Acts 16:30–31)?

_____

_____

b. The Bible says **Whoever calls on the name of the Lord shall be saved** (Romans 10:13). Based on what you have learned in the beginning statement in question #5, what do you think it means to call on the name of the Lord?

_____

_____

6. Shortly after Jesus' crucifixion the apostle Peter preached to a large group of people on the day of Pentecost (Acts 2:14–36). When Peter finished preaching, the audience said, **"Men and brethren, what shall we do?"** (Acts 2:37). Peter replied, **"Repent and be baptized"** (Acts 2:38). How do we know that baptism is *not* necessary for salvation?

1. Luke 23:39–43: _____

_____

2. 1 Corinthians 1:12–17: _____

_____

7. Jesus emphasized the importance of obeying His command to make disciples by saying, **"All authority has been given to Me in heaven and on earth"** (Matthew 28:18). If you are

a Christian, have you accepted Christ's authority over your life, including His command to make disciples?

❏ Yes   ❏ No
❏ Yes, but I don't know how to make disciples.

8. In Acts 1:8 Jesus introduces the word *witness* to expand the believer's understanding of his role and responsibility regarding the Great Commission (Acts 1:8). Why do you think the word *witness* is an appropriate term to describe a disciple of Jesus Christ?

    _____

    _____

    _____

9. In John 20:21 Jesus said: **"Peace to you, As the Father has sent Me, I also send you."** List two possible interpretations of Jesus' statement.

    1. _____

        _____

    2. _____

        _____

10. God's call to believers to be witnesses and preach the gospel to the world seems impossible, but they must obey His command. All believers face the same dilemma. Do I respond to God's call by saying, "I can't and I won't" or "I can't, but I must"? Englishman John Wesley (1703–1791) said, "I do not ask if it is compassable (comprehensible). I only ask if it is commanded." It's only when a believer acknowledges Christ's commission is a command and his inability to fulfill His command that he'll turn to God in faith and receive the grace he needs.

    a. Jesus knew His followers couldn't fulfill the Great Commission in their own strength and they would be

Is your study going well? Consider starting a new group. To learn how, go to www. Lamplighters USA.org/training.

———

ADDITIONAL INSIGHTS

tempted to reject His command. Jesus said He would give believers the **"Promise of My Father"** (Luke 24:49). What is the promise Jesus gives believers to enable them to fulfill His command (Acts 1:8)?

_____

_____

_____

_____

b. What do you think it means for a believer to appropriate the power of the Holy Spirit to fulfill the Great Commission?

_____

_____

_____

_____

FOUR

WHAT IS A DISCIPLE?

Read John 8:30; Luke 14:25–33; other references as given.

In the last lesson you learned the five New Testament references that comprise the Great Commission. You also learned that the "I can't, and I won't" versus "I can't, but I must" dilemma is solved when the believer learns to rely on the Holy Spirit's power to accomplish God's will. To appropriate this power from the Holy Spirit, you must (1) accept Christ's command as a personal mandate, (2) acknowledge your inability to fulfill the Great Commission in your own strength, and (3) trust the Holy Spirit to empower you as you step out in faith to obey Christ's command.

The word *disciple* appears 262 times in the Bible, while the word *Christian* appears only three times. The striking disparity of use of these two words teaches an important spiritual truth: God wants us to be and to make disciples of Jesus Christ, not merely casual converts or "Sunday-only Christians." In this lesson you'll learn (1) the three general ways the word *disciple* is used in the Bible, (2) the three different types of disciples who followed Jesus, and (3) the four characteristics of a true disciple.

Before you begin, ask God to reveal Himself to you and to transform you into the image of Jesus Christ.

1. Many Christians are confused about (1) what it means to be a disciple and (2) God's plan to make disciples. Unfortunately, this confusion keeps many believers from obeying God's

Gospel Gold Rule:

Try to get all the answers to the questions—not just the easy ones. Go for the gold.

ADD GROUP INSIGHTS BELOW

command, experiencing the joy of being used by Him, and fulfilling their purpose in life.

a. Are you a disciple? ❏ Yes   ❏ No   ❏ I am not sure.

b. Are you a disciple of Jesus Christ?
❏ Yes   ❏ No
❏ I am not sure. What kind of disciple do you mean?

2. A disciple (Greek *mathetes*) is a learner or follower of another. A disciple is under the discipline or training of another. The word can be used in a general, non-Christian way (Plato was a disciple of Socrates) or a religious sense (Acts 16:1). List the three general types of disciples in the Bible.

1. John 9:28: _____

_____

2. Matthew 11:2: _____

_____

3. Matthew 8:19–22: _____

_____

3. The word *disciple* refers to three different groups of followers in the New Testament, including (unsaved) Jewish followers of the Law of Moses and the disciples of John the Baptist. When Jesus said, **"Go and make disciples"** (Matthew 28:19), He was obviously referring to a third group—those who professed a willingness to be His disciples. Jesus, however, realized that not all of His disciples truly understood the cost of discipleship. Briefly describe two types of Jesus' disciples who did *not* understand the type of followers Jesus wanted.

1. Matthew 8:19–22: _____

_____

2. John 6:60–66: _____

_____

4. What do you think Jesus meant when He said, **"He who eats My flesh and drinks My blood abides in Me, and I in him. As the living Father sent Me, and I live because of the Father, so he who feeds on Me will live because of Me"** (John 6:56–57)?

_____

_____

_____

Balance Rule:

To learn how to balance the group discussion, go to www.Lamplighters USA.org/training.

ADDITIONAL INSIGHTS

5. Jesus didn't chase after those disciples who felt the cost of discipleship was too great. Jesus also didn't pander to their "felt needs" or soften His message to gain a following by appealing to their selfish ways.

   a. Jesus let these carnal disciples go and turned to the twelve and asked, **"Do you also want to go away?"** (John 6:67). Peter gave the quintessential (ideal, classic) response that every true disciple should be able to give at a moment's notice. What did Peter say in response to Jesus' question (John 6:68)?

   _____

   _____

   b. If Jesus told you that following Him meant giving up your life, what would you do? Would you go away or say like Peter, **"Lord, to whom shall we go? You have the words of eternal life"** (John 6:68)?

   Why? _____

   _____

   _____

   _____

6. You've learned that the word *disciple* refers to three types of followers: (1) unsaved followers of the Law of Moses (John 9:28), (2) followers of John the Baptist (Matthew 11:2), (3)

those who choose earthly priorities over following Jesus (Matthew 8:19–22) and those who want the benefits of following Jesus without the challenges of being His faithful followers (John 6:60–66).

a. When Jesus commanded the apostles, **"Go and make disciples"** (Matthew 28:18–20), He was not instructing the apostles to make any of the disciples listed above. He wants something more from His followers. But when Jesus commanded the apostles to make disciples (Matthew 28:18–20), He didn't explain the type of disciple He wanted them to make. How do you think the apostles knew what type of disciple Jesus wanted if He didn't tell them when He gave the Great Commission?

_____

_____

_____

b. In Matthew 28:19 Jesus gave His apostles a skeletal outline of the discipleship process. They were to make disciples by winning the lost to Christ (assumed) and baptizing those who trusted Christ in the name of the Father, Son, and Holy Spirit. What else are Jesus' followers to do to complete the process of making disciples of all nations (Matthew 28:20)?

_____

_____

_____

_____

7. Perhaps you struggled to answer part "a" of the previous question, but the answer is amazingly simple. Jesus had already taught the apostles the four qualifications of a true disciple. In fact, Jesus was so clear about the characteristics of a true disciple that it's likely that the apostles instinctively knew what He meant when He said, **"Go and make disciples"** (Matthew 28:19).

a. In John 8:31 Jesus said, **"If you abide in My word, you are My disciples indeed."** Many translations translate the phrase *My disciples* with an emphasis in the adjective ("true disciples" [NASB], "truly my disciples" [ESV, Phillips, TLB, MSG], "you really are My disciples" [NIV, Holman]). Jesus was qualifying the kind of disciple that He was looking for. What do you think it means for a Christian to abide in God's Word?

_____

_____

_____

b. In Luke 14:26–33 Jesus presents three additional characteristics of a true disciple. What do you think is the meaning of this second characteristic of a true disciple (Luke 14:26)?

_____

_____

_____

c. Jesus presented the third qualification of a true disciple in Luke 14:27. Since only Jesus could bear His cross and the sin of the world, He was not referring to His own passion at the crucifixion. What do you think it means for a believer to **bear his cross and come after Me (Jesus)**?

_____

_____

_____

d. The fourth and final qualification of a true or convicted disciple of Jesus Christ is found in Luke 14:33. What do you think it means for a true disciple to **forsake all that he has** (Luke 14:33; Matthew 19:27–30; Colossians 3:1–3)?

It's time to choose your next study. Turn to the back of the study guide for a list of available studies or go online for the latest studies.

ADDITIONAL
INSIGHTS

_____

_____

_____

_____

8. The word *disciple* has a range of meaning. It can refer to an unsaved religious adherent of a religious system, someone who is a casual associate of Jesus Christ, or a true follower of Jesus Christ.

   a. The question is not whether you are a disciple of Jesus, but what kind of disciple of Jesus you are. Are you a casual disciple or follower of Christ, one who is looking for the blessings that Jesus provides but flees when God allows challenges into your life, or a true disciple?

     _____

     _____

   b. What changes, if any, could you make in your life to become a true disciple of Jesus Christ?

     _____

     _____

     _____

     _____

     _____

     _____

     _____

FIVE

WHAT ARE THE PRINCIPLES OF DISCIPLESHIP?

Read references as given.

In the last lesson you learned the various ways the word *disciple* is used in the Bible and the kind of disciple Jesus was looking for when He said, **"Go and make disciples"** (Matthew 28:19). Most importantly, I hope you learned the four characteristics of a true disciple of Jesus Christ.

In this lesson you'll learn seven disciple-making principles that were modeled by Jesus Christ and replicated by the early church. Each principle is presented as a statement (*italic print*) that is followed by a brief explanation. Questions are asked to help you learn these disciple-making truths directly from Scripture. These seven principles are the basis of the Intentional Discipleship Bible Study (IDBS) method of disciple-making. To learn more about IDBS, including how to start an IDBS ministry in your church or community, contact Lamplighters International. A discipleship trainer will answer your questions and guide you in the training process.

Before you begin, ask God to reveal Himself to you and to transform you into the image of Jesus Christ.

1. Principle #1: *A disciple-maker helps others understand God's will, but he doesn't try to run their lives.* Jesus and the early church leaders (Paul) were not afraid to tell others God's will (Matthew 5:21–22, 38–39; Ephesians 6:5–6; 1 Thessalonians 4:3–4), but they refused to make their personal convictions a focus of their discipleship.

Many groups study the Final Exam the week after the final lesson for three reasons: (1) someone might come to Christ, (2) believers gain assurance of salvation, (3) group members learn how to share the gospel.

ADD GROUP INSIGHTS BELOW

a. What did Jesus tell the Pharisees they had done wrong in their attempt to follow God and teach others (Matthew 23:23–24)?

_____

_____

b. In Acts 15 the apostles gathered to determine if non-Jewish (Gentile) believers should be included in the church. The Jewish apostles could have required the Gentiles to keep some or all of the Old Testament Law of Moses, but they didn't. How does their final recommendation to the Gentile believers demonstrate (1) a careful concern to obey God's Word and (2) an unwillingness to make their personal convictions a test of fellowship (Acts 15:24–29)?

_____

_____

_____

_____

c. As a disciple-maker, you can confidently instruct younger believers to obey God's Word, but you must be careful not to violate matters of their Christian conscience. What word of caution did Paul give the Roman believers regarding this issue (Romans 14:1–12)?

_____

_____

_____

_____

2. Principle #2: *A disciple-maker helps others understand the "Three Deaths" of the believer.* Christians understand that Christ died for them (Romans 5:8, first death). Some Christians understand they died with Christ (Galatians 2:20,

second death), but even fewer believers understand what Paul meant when he said, **"I die daily"** (1 Corinthians 15:31).

a. It has been said that the church should be teaching believers how to die to self rather than how to live for Christ. Just as in the physical realm, life is always born out of death. What do you think Jesus meant when He said, **"Unless a grain of wheat falls into the ground and dies, it remains alone; but if it dies, it produces much grain. He who loves his life will lose it, and he who hates his life in this world will keep it for eternal life"** (John 12:24–25)?

_____

_____

_____

b. If Christ died for us (first death) and Paul said, **"I have been crucified with Him"** (Galatians 2:20, the second death), what did Paul mean when he said, **"I die daily"** (1 Corinthians 15:31)?

_____

_____

_____

c. If you are a Christian, do you say each morning, "I want to live for God today," or "I want to die to self (my desires, my pleasures) today that Christ might live through me"?

_____

3. Principle #3: *A disciple-maker always trains leaders as he teaches others.* Jesus trained His disciples as He taught the multitudes (Mark 4:1–11), and Paul trained his missionary companions (Timothy, Titus, et al.) as he evangelized the world.

a. List four ways Jesus trained the apostles, His next generation of spiritual leaders.

Transformation
Rule:

Seek for personal transformation, not mere information, from God's Word.

———

ADDITIONAL
INSIGHTS

1. Mark 1:17: _____

_____

2. John 17:9, 14: _____

_____

3. Mark 6:7–12: _____

_____

4. Mark 6:34–44: _____

_____

b. How did Paul train leaders as they taught others (Acts 16:1–3; 20:20–28; 1 Timothy 1:1–3; 2 Timothy 3:10; Philemon 1–3)?

_____

_____

4. Principle #4: *A disciple-maker relies on God's Word and the Holy Spirit to be the primary agents of spiritual transformation.* A disciple-maker helps others understand God's Word and how to respond to the guidance of the Holy Spirit.

a. In John 18, Pontius Pilate asked a classic question: **"What is truth?"** (John 18:38). What is the answer to this important question and what will the truth do for you (John 17:17)?

_____

_____

b. What is another name for the Holy Spirit, and what do you think is the meaning of the phrase **He will guide you into all truth** (John 16:13)?

_____

5. Principle #5: *A disciple-maker doesn't chase after those who need to be discipled but who are unwilling to be discipled.* Jesus and Paul ministered to all who would listen. Both

Jesus and Paul were relentless in their desire to reach the lost, but they didn't chase after those who were unwilling to follow Him.

No-Trespassing
Rule:

To keep the Bible
study on track,
avoid talking
about political
parties, church
denominations,
and Bible
translations.

ADDITIONAL
INSIGHTS

a. What instruction did Jesus give the apostles when He sent them out on their first missionary journey (Matthew 10:11–14)?

_____

_____

b. What did Paul say to the Jews at Corinth when they rejected the truth (Acts 18:6)?

_____

_____

6. Principle #6: *A disciple-maker lives with a sense of spiritual urgency for believers to be perfected in Christ and the lost to be saved.* Jesus' death on the cross revealed His passion, and Paul bore in his body the marks of the Lord Jesus (Galatians 6:17). Both wore the scars of their zeal for an eternal mission.

a. How did Jesus demonstrate His intense desire for the lost to be saved and believers to be perfected in the faith (Luke 19:10; 23:44–46; John 17:8–9)?

_____

_____

_____

b. Paul's preaching at Derbe brought conviction of sin on the people who stoned him and left him for dead (Acts 14:19–20). When God raised him up, he went back into the city. What did Paul also say to the Galatian believers that demonstrated his intense desire for the spiritual advancement of others (Galatians 4:19)?

_____

_____

c. On a scale of 1 to 10 (1 being apathy and 10 being intense desire), what number would you give yourself regarding your desire to see others come to a saving knowledge of Jesus Christ? _____

On a scale of 1 to 10 (1 being apathy and 10 being intense desire), what number would you give yourself regarding your desire to see other Christians come to spiritual maturity in Christ? _____

7. Principle #7: *A disciple-maker prays for God to raise up laborers (disciples) because the harvest is plentiful.* Jesus spent long hours in prayer, and Paul prayed for the churches (Ephesians 1:15–23) and asked others to pray that he would proclaim the gospel as he ought (Ephesians 6:18–20).

   a. Why did Jesus command His followers to pray for more laborers (Matthew 9:37–38)?

   _____

   _____

   _____

   b. What did Paul ask the Ephesian believers to pray on his behalf (Ephesians 6:20)?

   _____

   _____

   _____

8. Which of the seven principles of disciple-making did you find the most enlightening and helpful?

   _____

   _____

   _____

   _____

   _____

SIX

SO WHAT'S THE HURRY?

Read references as given.

Our study on discipleship has led us to understand God's master plan that includes His call to believers to join Him to help all people submit to the Lord Jesus Christ in all things. The Great Commission is so comprehensive from man's perspective that it's impossible to carry out without the power of the Holy Spirit. You learned that the word *disciple* refers to a wide variety of people (saved and unsaved) in the Bible, but Jesus is looking for followers who manifest the four characteristics of true disciples.

In our final study you will learn what the Bible says about the urgency of reaching people for Christ. Many Christians are genuinely concerned about their lost family members, friends, and coworkers, but their concern never rises to a level of spiritual urgency. In this final lesson you'll learn that a casual concern for the lost is an enemy of the disciple-maker that prevents him from fulfilling the Great Commission.

Before you begin this lesson, ask God to reveal Himself to you and to transform you into the image of Jesus Christ with a sense of urgency to reach the lost.

1. a. What happens to those who die in their sins (Luke 16:22–23; Revelation 20:11–15)?

   _____

   _____

   _____

It's time to order your next study. Allow enough time to get the books so you can distribute them at the Open House. Consider ordering 2-3 extra books for newcomers.

———

ADD GROUP INSIGHTS BELOW

ADDITIONAL
INSIGHTS

b. What happens to those who have placed their complete trust in Jesus Christ alone for eternal life (Romans 10:13; 1 Peter 1:3–4)?

_____

_____

2. a. There are only two types of people in this world; those who are saved and those who are lost. Every day we interact with those who are destined for eternity with God and those who will face everlasting separation from God. Why do you think so many Christians lack a sense of urgency to reach the lost for Christ?

_____

_____

b. How badly does it bother you that some of your friends and family are lost and separated from God and will be eternally lost unless they are saved? Choose the statements that reflect your attitude about reaching the lost for Christ.

❑ I really don't think about it.
❑ It bothers me a lot.
❑ I try not to think about it.
❑ It bothers me, but I can't do anything about it.
❑ I really don't care. It's their decision.
❑ It bothers me, and I think the church should do more to reach them.

3. God is so concerned about the eternal destiny of the unsaved that He gave His only Son to die to pay for their redemption. What does the Bible say about the extent of God's concern for man's salvation?

1. Ezekiel 33:11: _____

_____

2. 2 Peter 3:9: _____

Final Exam:

Are you meeting next week to study the Final Exam? To learn how to present it effectively, contact Lamplighters.

ADDITIONAL INSIGHTS

4. Jesus' desire to reach the lost is illustrated when He led His disciples on a dangerous mission. Jesus and the apostles traveled directly north from Jerusalem to Samaria to present the gospel to a woman (John 4:1). The normal route from Jerusalem to Galilee in the north was to go east along the Jericho road to the Jordan River and up the Jordan River valley to Galilee. The direct route over the rugged Judean mountains was both strenuous and dangerous.

    a. What happened at the city of Sychar that revealed Jesus' passion to reach the lost (John 4:6–26, 39–42)?

    _____

    _____

    b. David Brainerd (1718–1747), missionary to the American Indians during colonial days, said, "I cared not how or where I lived or what hardships I endured, so that I could but gain souls for Christ." What did Jesus say to His disciples to help them understand the urgency of reaching people with the gospel (John 4:35)?

    _____

    _____

5. It is likely that the apostles passed this same woman on their way into the city. Whether it was ethnic prejudice, a lack of compassion for the lost, or some other reason that kept them from being concerned about her eternal destiny, we'll never know. We know, however, that in a short time this woman, whose life had been ravaged by sin, was transformed by Christ.

    a. What did Jesus say about the number of people who could be saved (Matthew 9:37–38)?

    _____

    _____

b. What did Jesus say about the number of religious people who will be eternally lost (Matthew 7:21–23)?

_____

_____

6. John Wesley said, "If I had three hundred men who feared nothing but God, hated nothing but sin, and were determined to know nothing among men but Jesus Christ and Him crucified, I would set the world on fire." What are three things you could do to become a more effective witness for Jesus Christ?

1. _____

_____

2. _____

_____

3. _____

_____

7. Review:

a. What is God's master plan (Ephesians 1:7–10)?

_____

_____

_____

b. What is the Great Commission?

_____

_____

c. What are the four characteristics of a true disciple of Jesus Christ?

1. _____

2. _____

3. _____

4. _____

Would you like to learn how to lead someone through this same study? It's not hard. Go to www.Lamplighters USA.org to register for *free* online leadership training.

ADDITIONAL INSIGHTS

8. Complete this final exercise from memory to test your understanding about biblical discipleship. Underline your answers. More than one answer could apply in the parentheses.

To be an effective disciple-maker, I must obey Christ's **(command, suggestion)**, which is repeated **(4-5-6)** times in Scripture by making **(converts, church members, true disciples, denominational adherents)** of Jesus Christ of all **(Americans, people I like, Westerners, nations)**. I will do this by **(wearing a cross, testifying as His witness, accepting God's call to be His ambassador and a faithful witness, having a fish bumper sticker, going to church)** and **(inviting people to church, proclaiming the gospel, voting family values)**. The Gospel is **(God loves me and has a wonderful plan for my life; praying the "Sinner's Prayer"; Christ's death, burial, and resurrection and my response of repentance and belief in Christ's finished work which results in forgiveness of my sins)**. To fulfill Christ's mission, I must **(build more churches, become busier in Christian ministry, become more politically active, follow Christ's and the early church's pattern of making disciples, give more money to missions)** and **(encourage my church leaders to do more, ask God to give me a different personality, pray for the gift of evangelism, take college classes on assertiveness, learn to rely on the Holy Spirit's power, invent new tricks and gimmicks to share the gospel, learn to use Twitter and Facebook)** and trust that Christ will never leave me. I must **(teach, train, encourage)** new believers to obey **(some, a few, most, all, a majority) of** the things Christ commanded in His Word.

9. What are the most important truths you learned from this study on discipleship?

LEADER'S GUIDE

Lesson 1: Is There a Word from the Lord?

1. a. **"There is."**
   b. Answers will vary.

2. a. Answers will vary, but the Bible is what it claims to be, God's inerrant revelation.
   b. 2 Timothy 3:16: The Bible says all Scripture is God-breathed (Greek *theopneustos*, "inspired"). God's words were given through men who were superintended by the Holy Spirit so that their writings are without error.
   2 Peter 1:20–21: The Scriptures did not originate in the minds of the prophets themselves, but they were given by God through the superintending ministry of the Holy Spirit. Since the Holy Spirit is without error or fault, the Scriptures are also without error.

3. When Jesus said **the Scripture cannot be broken** (John 10:35), He was saying all the Scriptures are without error. This is a powerful statement about the inerrancy of the Bible that refutes the argument that the Bible contains the words of God and the words of man.

4. 1. Fulfilled prophecy. Jeremiah 28:9 says, **As for the prophet who prophesies of peace, when the word of the prophet comes to pass, the prophet will be known as one whom the LORD has truly sent.** Hundreds of prophecies have come to pass exactly as they were prophesied, proving that the Lord truly sent the prophets to speak in His name. Many of these prophecies are amazingly specific (Isaiah 52:13–53:12; Micah 5:2), providing ample proof of the supernatural character of the Scriptures.
   2. Archeology. Archeological discoveries have repeatedly confirmed the accuracy of the geography of the Bible.
   3. Unity of the Bible. The books of the Bible were written over a period of 1,500 years by a variety of authors with a wide range of backgrounds (kings, a government official, a farmer, prophets, shepherds, fishermen, etc.), most of whom never met each other. Yet the Bible manifests

a unity of theme and a consistency that can only be explained as supernaturally inspired by God.

4. Jesus and the New Testament writers' testimonies about Scripture. Jesus said not one word of the Old Testament Law would pass away (not even the smallest letter or part of a letter; Matthew 5:18) until all is fulfilled. Jesus authenticated the historical account of Jonah and the fish (Matthew 12:40). The New Testament writers quoted from the Old Testament repeatedly as support for the theological truths they were writing about. The apostle Paul said all Scripture was inspired by God (2 Timothy 3:16).

5. a. 1. The Bible teaches us how to live right. (It is profitable for doctrine/teaching)
   2. The Bible teaches us where we went wrong. (It is profitable for reproof)
   3. The Bible teaches us how to get back on the right path. (It is profitable for correction)
   4. The Bible instructs us how to stay on the right path in life. (It is profitable for training in righteousness)
   b. The Christian will be completely (thoroughly) equipped to live a God-honoring life.
   c. Answers will vary.

6. God has given to us all things that pertain to life and godliness. This enablement in a believer's life is directly related to his knowledge of God who called him by His glory and virtue (2 Peter 1:3). God, in His infinite wisdom, has provided everything a believer needs to live a God-honoring life, including all he needs to fulfill the Great Commission.

7. Answers will vary, but all the answers should be "yes."

8. a. 1. A greater love for self than a love for God
   2. A lack of conviction. Many believers do not think God's commands are authoritative
   3. A lack of training
   4. Fear of failure
   5. Discipleship requires more than teaching. It requires training. Jesus said, **"Follow Me and I will make you fishers of men."** (Mark 1:17)

6. A disciple-making mind-set has not been normalized in many churches.
   Other answers could apply.
   b. Answers will vary.

9. Answers will vary.

10. Answers will vary.

Lesson 2: Does God Have a Plan?

1. 1. Jesus came to seek those who are lost (Luke 19:10).
   2. Jesus came to give us an example of how to live (John13:12–15; 1 Peter 2:21).
   3. Jesus came to destroy the works of the devil (1 John 3:8).

2. Answers will vary. God's grand plan is to bring everything together under the sovereign authority of Jesus Christ (Ephesians 1:10). Believers work together with Him as His fellow-laborers (1 Corinthians 3:9) to accomplish His master plan. Since God is sovereign and omnipotent (all-powerful), He doesn't need believers to help Him, but He graciously invites them to join this great missional endeavor.

3. a. Farmer/gardener — to plant (the gospel in the hearts of people, evangelism) and to water (nurturing young believers in the truth)
   b. Wise builder — to work carefully and wisely to build God's truth into the lives of all people
   c. Individual parts of a human body — to be unified as a whole; to honor and respect other members of the body of Christ
   d. Chosen nation, Royal priesthood, Holy nation, a special people. — to proclaim God's excellencies and praises
   e. Sojourners, aliens — to abstain from fleshly desires and live honorably among the unsaved

4. a. The individual is transferred from the domain of darkness to the kingdom of God's dear Son.
   b. A citizen of heaven.
   c. God gives the new believer a grand new mission or purpose in life. As a citizen of heaven, the believer should do all he can to reconcile the lost to God and help those who are saved to fully embrace Jesus Christ's supremacy in all aspects of their lives.

5. 1. Both serve at the will of a higher authority.
   2. Both serve in a foreign land.
   3. Both must be careful to represent their sovereign will in all areas of conduct.
   4. Both must not speak on their own authority.
      Other answers could apply.

6. a. They viewed themselves as strangers and pilgrims on the earth.
   b. Answers will vary.
   c. 1. They wanted a better country/city (Hebrews 11:8–10).
      2. They wanted a better country (Hebrews 11:13–16).
      3. They wanted a better resurrection (Hebrews 11:35).
   d. Answers will vary.

7. 1. The veil in the temple was torn in two from top to bottom (Matthew 27:51).
   2. The earth quaked, and the rocks split (Matthew 27:51).
   3. Graves in Jerusalem were opened, and many people were raised (Matthew 27:52). After Jesus' resurrection, those who were resurrected came out of the graves and went into Jerusalem and were seen by many people (Matthew 27:53).

8. Christians have direct access to God through Jesus Christ. This should transform a believer's prayer-life and inspire him to work together with God to bring all things under the authority of Jesus Christ. The believer can do this in all aspects of his life (home, work, etc.). He doesn't need anyone's permission to fulfill the ministry God has given him.

9. Answers will vary.

Lesson 3: Great Commission or Great Confusion?

1. a. 1. Isaiah 53:6: All people have turned away from God to their own way.
   2. Romans 3:12: All people have turned away from God and become useless (unprofitable) to Him. There is nobody who doesn't fit into this category.
   3. Romans 3:19: All people are guilty before God.
   4. Ephesians 2:1, 12: All people are (spiritually) dead to God because of their trespasses and sins. They don't have a relationship with Jesus Christ, and they are like strangers to the blessings that God has given Israel and they have no access (strangers) to God's promises. They have no hope within themselves of having a relationship with God unless He intervenes in their lives. They are without God in this world—the only One who can give meaning and hope to their lives.

   b. The lost (unsaved) person stands before God, and he is judged by his works. Having died in his sins, he has no chance of "secondary redemption" at the Great White Throne judgment. His judgment of works only reveals the degree of his eternal punishment.

2. 1. The sheer magnitude of the Great Commission proves that Christ's command includes all believers. To preach or proclaim the Good News to all the world and make disciples of all nations requires a worldwide effort on the part of all believers.
   2. Paul wasn't present when the Great Commission was given, but he believed he was under obligation to preach the gospel to Jews and to non-Jews (Gentiles). What was this obligation? It was the Great Commission that Jesus gave to the original apostles, which applies to all believers of all ages.

3. The Bible says those who were persecuted went everywhere preaching the Word. Since the apostles stayed in Jerusalem, those who spread the Word were "lay" believers. Nothing is said about these believers being a particular group of believers within the church or that they possessed some special gift of evangelism.

4. a. Strictly speaking, the gospel is Jesus Christ's death, burial, and

resurrection that's able to save a person when he receives Christ's finished sacrifice on his behalf as complete payment for his sins (1 Corinthians 15:1–4). Anyone who believes the gospel is saved or born again. Though he's been separated and alienated from God, he has been restored through salvation. In a broader context, the word *gospel* refers to the entire message of God, including the need for complete faith in Him and His promise of redemption (Hebrews 4:2).

    b. 1. Yes. Praying a prayer does not save an individual. An individual must come under the conviction of the Holy Spirit and trust Jesus Christ for eternal life.

       2. Yes. See the answer to question #6 below.

       3. Yes. An individual is saved by grace, not works (Ephesians 2:8–9).

       4. Yes. An individual is saved individually (John 1:12). A general belief in the person of Jesus Christ will not save an individual. The Bible says even the demons believe — and tremble (James 2:19).

       5. Yes. An individual is saved when he believes in Jesus Christ alone for eternal life. When an individual says, "I asked Jesus into my heart," he may truly be saved, but his statement is unclear and it is probably confusing to an unsaved person.

5. a. **"Believe on the Lord Jesus Christ, and you will be saved, you and your household."**

    b. To call on the name of the Lord means to believe/trust that Jesus Christ's sacrifice on the cross can be personally applied to an individual's life, resulting in the individual's eternal salvation.

6. 1. Luke 23:39–43: When the thief who died with Jesus asked Him to remember him, Jesus told him that he would be with Him in Paradise (Luke 23:43). Jesus does not say anything about the need for baptism.

    2. 1 Corinthians 1:12–17: Paul told the Corinthians that God did not send him to baptize people, but to preach the gospel (1 Corinthians 1:17). In this passage Paul clearly separates the gospel from baptism. Paul, however, isn't saying that baptism is not important. He is saying that baptizing believers was not the primary focus of his ministry. The importance of baptism in the disciple-making process is highlighted by its inclusion in the Great Commission (Matthew 28:19).

7. Answers will vary.

8   The phrase **"you shall be witnesses"** (Acts 1:8) can be interpreted two ways: (1) as a command (go and be witnesses) or (2) as a statement of fact. Either way, the apostles (and all believers by application) were to testify by word and action that Jesus was the Christ and the Savior of the world. They were not just to live God-honoring lives; they were to testify of Jesus' death, burial, and resurrection that saves man from his sin. The idea of being a silent witness ("I will let my life be my witness") is absent from Jesus' statement. A witness in a court of law testifies by his or her words. The quote "Preach the gospel, and if necessary, use words," perhaps incorrectly credited to Francis of Assisi, has been used to satisfy the conscience of many who are reluctant to be vocal witnesses for Christ, but the statement is not supported by Scripture.

9. 1.   Jesus is saying that God the Father sent Him, and He (Jesus) is now sending or commissioning them. Jesus accepted His Father's commission and He is now officially transferring His commission to them. If this is the correct interpretation, Jesus' words convey a strong military sense. Military officers transfer their commissions to new officers during official commissioning services.

    2.   Jesus is instructing His disciples that they should follow His pattern of disciple-making. Just as He made disciples, they should make disciples (**"As the Father has sent Me** [to make disciples]", follow My example and do it the same way"). This second possible interpretation offers a strong recommendation to study the life of Christ to learn how He discipled others. Jesus said, **"Follow Me, and I will make you become fishers of men"** (Mark 1:17).

10. a.   God promises to give all believers the power of the Holy Spirit so they can fulfill the Great Commission.

    b.   This means God in the person of the Holy Spirit gives the believer (1) spiritual courage to step out on faith to obey Christ's Great Commission, (2) wisdom to know how to engage those who need Christ, and (3) the words of truth to lead others to fully embrace their God-given identity in Christ.

Lesson 4: What Is a Disciple?

1. a. Answers will vary.
   b. Answers will vary.

2. 1. John 9:28: A disciple of Moses and a follower of the Old Testament Law.
   2. Matthew 11:2: A disciple or follower of John the Baptist.
   3. Matthew 8:19–22: A disciple of Jesus Christ.

3. 1. Matthew 8:19–22: These "disciples" didn't understand that following Jesus meant making His will and His commands their first priority. They wanted to follow Jesus, but only if it didn't interfere with their pursuit of their human relationships and earthly priorities.
   2. John 6:60–66: These "disciples" didn't understand that there is a cost associated with being a faithful follower of Jesus. Following Jesus means death to self and the self-directed life. It also means bearing the reproach of Jesus Christ. Jesus said, **"If the world hates you, you know that it hated Me before it hated you"** (John 15:18).

4. Jesus' reference to eating His flesh and drinking His blood was a bold statement that was designed to shock His shallow listeners out of their false concept of being disciples. The Jews were prohibited from eating blood (Leviticus 3:17; 17:10–14), but they also knew that blood was the means of their atonement. Jesus powerfully connected these two truths to cause them to question their "theology." Jesus was saying that He was their "spiritual manna." Just as God gave manna to their forefathers during the Exodus to sustain their physical lives (Exodus 16:35; Numbers 11:6–8), God gave Jesus to be spiritual manna to give them eternal life. Jesus' blood is also spiritual drink. God gave their forefathers water from the rock, and it gave them physical life; Jesus' drink (His blood) was eternal life. Jesus was saying that the only way to live (eternally) is to fully accept His spiritual food (His body/flesh) and drink (His blood) as payment for their sin.

5. a. **"Lord, to whom shall we go? You have the words of eternal life. Also, we have come to believe and know that You are the Christ, the Son of the living God."**
   b. Answers will vary.

6. a. Jesus clearly identified four characteristics of a true disciple earlier in His ministry (John 8:31; Luke 14:25–33). Since Jesus regularly taught in the presence of His disciples and traveled with them for three and a half years, it's safe to assume that His disciples knew what He meant when He said, **"Go and make disciples"** (Matthew 28:18–20).

   b. Jesus' followers are to train (**[teach] them to *observe* all things**) their disciples to do all things Christ commanded (Matthew 28:20). In the ancient world, teaching meant that the disciple understood the truth being trained to the point of doing. The modern idea of knowing to the point of reciting but not doing is foreign to the concept of ancient teaching and true discipleship. This truth (teaching versus training/ teaching to observe) has profound implications for all aspects of Christian ministry.

7. a. Jesus' encouraging words imply His disciples were already abiding or remaining in His Word/truth. For a disciple to abide or remain in Jesus, he is living/walking in fellowship with Him, trusting Him and His promises, and living in obedience to the truth God has revealed to him. Abiding in Christ means even though God has not revealed all truth to the disciple, he is being obedient to the truth God has revealed at this point in his spiritual journey. This verse helps believers understand two important truths about abiding in Christ: (1) It is possible to abide in Christ or walk with Him, and (2) Those who walk with God (abide in Him) shouldn't allow themselves to be plagued with guilt over things God has not yet revealed to them.

   b. A true disciple of Jesus makes his relationship with Him more important than anything else, including his own life and his closest human relationships. Although this verse appears confusing at first glance, the verse is easily understood when you learn that there is no comparative or superlative (good, better, best) in the Hebrew language. In the Hebrew language, comparison was made between two objects of possible affection to show the "superiority" of one. Jesus, a Jew, used this Hebrew linguistic tool (even though He may have been speaking Greek or Aramaic) to demonstrate that a disciple's love for Him must supersede all other "loves," including the closest family members and one's own life. To do otherwise disqualifies one from being a true disciple of Jesus.

c. A true disciple of Jesus is willing to trust Him daily and especially during life's most difficult challenges and trials. When Jesus bore His cross, He said, **"Not as I will, but as You will"** (Matthew 26:39). This expression of submission to God should be the mantra of every believer. A second thought may also be in view in this verse. During a crucifixion, Rome required the condemned to carry his cross to the place of crucifixion. This action of carrying the cross indicated to bystanders that Rome was right to condemn the man and his guilt was established. When a Christian trusts Jesus during his trials, he is saying that Christ is right, and he will honor Him no matter the cost. To do this, the disciple is encouraged to count the cost of bearing his cross and honoring Christ (Luke 14:28–32). Again, to do otherwise disqualifies one from being a true disciple.

d. A true disciple must be willing to voluntarily relinquish all he owns and accept his rightful role as steward of God's possession (Psalm 24). The Bible says no man can serve two masters, for **either he will hate the one and love the other, or else he will be loyal to the one and despise the other. You cannot serve God and mammon** (Matthew 6:24). The believer who does not understand this truth will routinely pursue the things of the world. In doing so, he is not forsaking all that he has. This fourth characteristic of a true disciple is not promoting an ascetic lifestyle. An individual can have very little material wealth, but he still may not be willing to forsake (surrender to God) the things he has. Paul attacked the Colossian church's willingness to embrace asceticism, saying that it was not the path to true spiritual maturity (Colossians 2:20–24).

8. a. Answers will vary.
   b. Answers will vary.

Lesson 5: What Are the Principles of Discipleship?

1. a. The Pharisees had lost sight of the things of God that are of primary importance. They had replaced (neglected) the fundamental truths of justice, mercy, faith) with their desire to tithe even the smallest seeds. Jesus didn't say that they shouldn't tithe these things, He was saying their misplaced focus led them to forsake God and His ways. In the

same way, believers, churches, and denominations can fall prey to this same error. As a disciple-maker, focus on the truth of God's Word, and allow each one to come to personal conviction on his own. There is always the temptation to make others your disciples rather than disciples of Jesus Christ. Remember the word of John the Baptist: **"He must increase, but I must decrease"** (John 3:30).

b. The apostles believed the Holy Spirit wanted them to lay on the Gentile believers **no greater burden than these necessary things** (Acts 15:28). In the context, this is an amazing statement and an example of the apostles not laying on the Gentiles anything other than what God wanted. The Gentile believers were to abstain from idols, from blood, from things strangled, and from immorality (Acts 15:29). The prohibitions had to do with things that would hinder their witness within a pagan culture or were a clear violation of a scriptural prohibition.

c. Paul said some matters of Christian experience are issues of personal conviction, and believers should not judge others regarding them. We need to discern between personal scruples and fundamental biblical truths (inerrancy of the Scriptures, salvation by grace, Christ's bodily resurrection, etc.), which are nonnegotiables for the believer. Other issues, such as eating out on Sundays, types of music in the church, etc., are secondary issues and should not become a source of division among believers. A disciple-maker helps a disciple understand this distinction.

2. a. The wheat analogy illustrates a foundational spiritual truth—death is the path to life. Jesus' death led to eternal life for believers, and the disciple of Jesus must understand that he died with Christ (Romans 6:5–11). The disciple is to hate **his life in this world,** meaning the believer values his new life in Christ so much that he doesn't place any significant value on the things of this world. Life in this world is characterized by self-centered desires that only bring fleeting pleasure, frustration, and emptiness. **The man who loves his life will lose it,** meaning he loses his life in the sense he will waste it by pursuing the things that won't satisfy him. The man who pursues worldly things misses the entire point of life. In a real sense, he loses his life.

b. Even though Paul had been crucified with Christ, he still lived in a real world with real temptations. Paul realized that his sinful desires warred against God, and he had to consciously and deliberately die to the desires of the flesh each day (**I die daily**). Even though he was a mature believer, Paul realized that he was not sinless, and he was not beyond being tempted (Philippians 3:12–14).

   c. Answers will vary.

3. a. 1. Mark 1:17: Jesus trained the apostles by allowing them to be with Him and by giving them clear directions where He was leading them.

      2. John 17:9: Jesus trained the apostles by loving them and giving them all of God's words.

      3. Mark 6:7–12: Jesus trained the apostles by giving them spiritual responsibilities and allowed them to trust God for themselves. This revealed their level of faith at the time.

      4. Mark 6:34–44: Jesus trained the disciples by being willing to meet the needs of those in need and by trusting God to provide supernatural power in response to prayer. This event also revealed to the apostles their need to see life's events from a perspective of the supernatural.

  b. Acts 16:1–3: Like Jesus, Paul trained missionaries by allowing them to be with him.

Acts 20:20–28: Like Jesus, Paul trained his (Jesus') disciples by giving them the Word.

1 Timothy 1:1–3: Paul wrote words of encouragement and instructions to his disciples.

2 Timothy 3:10: Like Jesus, Paul modeled a godly life for disciples to pattern their lives after.

Philemon 1–3: Paul included his disciples in ministry and told them that he loved them.

4. a. God's Word is truth. God's Word is the means by which man is sanctified (set apart) for God.

  b. Spirit of truth. The Holy Spirit will guide you *in* all truth (better translation, NIV). The Holy Spirit does not speak on His own accord. The word *guides* (Greek *dodegeo*—to lead, to guide) is used as a figure of speech to indicate the Holy Spirit leads believers to the complete truth. A disciple-maker must help a disciple understand God's Word and teach him how to let the Holy Spirit guide him.

5. a. When the disciples entered a city, they were to inquire who was worthy and stay with the man (and his family) until they had completed their missionary work. If they found the man and his family to be worthy (hospitable, one who accepted the missionaries and Christ's message), they were to bless the man and his family and leave them with a blessing of peace (likely a prayer of peace). But if the man and his family were not worthy (of the Lord), perhaps becoming unhospitable and/or rejecting the message, the disciples were to depart and not return (**shake off the dust from your feet**). The peace that the disciples were to leave with the host would return to them since it was rejected by the host. Perhaps the shaking of the dust off their feet is an also indication that the host had failed to do one of the most basic duties performed toward a guest; that of washing their feet.
   b. **"Your blood be upon your own heads; I am clean. From now on I will go to the Gentiles."**

6. a. 1. The Bible says Jesus came to earth to seek and to save those who are lost (Luke 19:10).
      2. Jesus willingly died on a cross for sins He had not committed (Luke 23:44–46).
      3. Jesus gave His followers the very words that God the Father gave Him (John 17:8–9).
   b. Paul said that he labored over their spiritual growth (until Christ is formed in you) like he was a woman suffering labor pains.
   c. Answers will vary.

7. a. The harvest is plentiful and the laborers (committed followers of Jesus) are few. In these two verses Jesus says more laborers are needed to reach the large numbers of people who can be saved.
   b. Paul asked the Ephesian believers to pray for him so he would have the spiritual courage to proclaim the good news about Christ. He said he ought to proclaim the message, and he wanted the Ephesian believers to pray for him for courage to do what God had commissioned him to do. Believers should ask other Christians to do the same for them.

8. Answers will vary.

Lesson 6: So What's the Hurry?

1. a. When they die, they go to hell (Luke 16:22–23). At a later time, they stand before God at the Great White Throne judgment and are judged according to their works (Revelation 20:11–15). At the Great White Throne Judgment, no one will be saved. They stand before God to receive their eternal punishment according to their deeds. Believers stand before God at the Bema Seat of Christ (2 Corinthians 5:10). At this judgment, no believer will be lost (1 Corinthians 3:11–15).
    b. Those who place their complete trust in Jesus Christ alone for eternal life will be saved (Romans 10:13) and receive an incorruptible inheritance when they enter heaven (1 Peter 1:3–4).

2. a. Answers will vary, but could include apathy, sin, worldliness, selfishness, fear of rejection, etc.
    b. Answers will vary.

3. 1. Ezekiel 33:11: God said He has no pleasure in the one who dies, meaning He has no pleasure in the person who dies without the saving knowledge of Him.
    2. 2 Peter 3:9: God is not willing that any should perish. The Bible does not teach universalism—the false doctrine that teaches all people will eventually be saved based upon God's love and desire. While it is God's desire for man to be saved, and He made a way for his salvation through Jesus Christ, many will not be saved (Matthew 7:21–23).

4. a. Jesus went out of His way to talk with a woman who had had five husbands and was living in sin. Jesus talked with her, and she came to faith.
    b. Jesus told His disciples that they should not be complacent or cavalier about reaching the lost. He said, **"Do you not say, 'There are still four months and then comes the harvest'? Behold, I say to you, lift up your eyes and look at the fields, for they are already white for harvest!"** (John 4:35). In Matthew 9:37–38 Jesus emphasizes the bountifulness of the harvest (many can be saved). In John4:35 Jesus emphasizes the readiness of the harvest (white for harvest). In the Matthew passage Jesus emphasizes praying for more workers. In John 4:35, Jesus emphasized two things: (1) the need for a greater

degree of urgency among God's people to reach the lost and (2) the need for a greater alertness to those around us who would be willing to hear the gospel if someone is willing to talk to them about Christ.

5. a. The harvest (of souls) is plentiful.
   b. Many people, including many who are religious, will not be saved.

6. Answers will vary.

7. a. **And this is the plan: At the right time he will bring everything together under the authority of Christ—everything in heaven and on earth** (Ephesians 1:10).
   b. The Great Commission is Jesus' command to all believers to join Him to help all people submit to the Lord Jesus Christ in all things. God's call is personal. Every believer has been called to make disciples. God's call is authoritative. Jesus said, **"Go into all the world and preach the gospel"** (Mark 16:15). God's call is effective. His call to make disciples implies effective ministry through the power of the Holy Spirit. God's call is comprehensive. Jesus has all authority, and all believers are to make disciples of all nations and teach them to obverse all things (Matthew 28:20).
   c. 1. A true disciple abides in close fellowship with Jesus Christ (John 8:31).
      2. A true disciple loves Jesus more than anything else (Luke 14:25).
      3. A true disciple of Jesus is willing to trust Him daily and especially during life's most difficult challenges and trials.
      4. A true disciple must be willing to voluntarily relinquish all he owns and accept his rightful role as steward of God's possession.

8. To be an effective disciple-maker, I must obey Christ's **(command, suggestion)**, which is repeated **(4-5-6)** times in Scripture by making **(converts, church members, true disciples, denominational adherents)** of Jesus Christ of all **(Americans, people I like, Westerners, nations)**. I will do this by **(wearing a cross, testifying as His witness, accepting God's call to be His ambassador and a faithful witness, having a fish bumper sticker, going to church)** and **(inviting people to church, proclaiming the Gospel, voting family values)**. The Gospel is **(God loves me and has a wonderful plan for my life, praying the "Sinner's Prayer, Christ's**

death, burial, and resurrection and my response of repentance and belief in Christ's finished work which results in forgiveness of my sins). To fulfill Christ's mission, I must **(build more churches, become busier in Christian ministry, become more politically active, follow Christ's and the early church's pattern of making disciples, give more money to missions)** and **(encourage my church leaders to do more, ask God to give me a different personality, pray for the gift of evangelism, take college classes on assertiveness, learn to rely on the Holy Spirit's power, invent new tricks and gimmicks to share the gospel, learn to use Twitter and Facebook)** and trust that Christ will never leave me. I must **(teach, train, encourage)** new believers to obey **(some, a few, most, all, a majority)** the things Christ commanded in His Word.

9. Answers will vary.

FINAL EXAM

Every person will eventually stand before God in judgment—the final exam. The Bible says, ***And it is appointed for men to die once, but after this the judgment*** (Hebrews 9:27).

May I ask you a question? *If you died today, do you know for certain you would go to heaven?* I did not ask if you're religious or a church member, nor did I ask if you've had some encounter with God—a meaningful spiritual experience. I didn't even ask if you believe in God or angels or if you're trying to live a good life. The question I *am* asking is this: *If you died today, do you know for certain you would go to heaven?*

When you die, you will stand alone before God in judgment. You'll either be saved for all eternity, or you will be separated from God for all eternity in what the Bible calls the lake of fire (Romans 14:12; Revelation 20:11–15). Tragically, many religious people who believe in God are not going to be accepted by Him when they die.

> ***Many will say to Me in that day, "Lord, Lord, have we not prophesied in Your name, cast out demons in Your name, and done many wonders in Your name?" And then I will declare to them, "I never knew you; depart from Me, you who practice lawlessness!"*** (Matthew 7:22–23)

God loves you and wants you to go to heaven (John 3:16; 2 Peter 3:9). If you are not sure where you'll spend eternity, you are not prepared to meet God. God wants you to know for certain that you will go to heaven.

> ***Behold, now is the accepted time; behold, now is the day of salvation.*** (2 Corinthians 6:2)

The words ***behold*** and ***now*** are repeated because God wants you to know that you can be saved today. You do not need to hear those terrible words, ***Depart from Me ....*** Isn't that great news?

Jesus himself said, ***You must be born again*** (John 3:7). These aren't the words of a pastor, a church, or a particular denomination. They're the words of Jesus Christ himself. You *must* be born again (saved from eternal damnation) before you die; otherwise, it will be too late when you die! You can know for certain today that God will accept you into heaven when you die.

These things I have written to you who believe in the name of the Son of God, that you may know *that you have eternal life.*

(1 John 5:13)

The phrase *you may know* means that you can know for certain before you die that you will go to heaven. To be born again, you must understand and accept four essential spiritual truths. These truths are right from the Bible, so you know you can trust them—they are not man-made religious traditions. Now, let's consider these four essential spiritual truths.

Essential Spiritual Truth

#1

The Bible teaches that you are a sinner and separated from God.

No one is righteous in God's eyes. To be righteous means to be totally without sin, not even a single act.

There is none righteous, no, not one;
There is none who understands;
There is none who seeks after God.
They have all turned aside;
They have together become unprofitable;
There is none who does good, no, not one.
(Romans 3:10–12)

...for all have sinned and fall short of the glory of God.
(Romans 3:23)

Look at the words God uses to show that all men are sinners—**none, not one, all turned aside, not one**. God is making a point: all of us are sinners. No one is good (perfectly without sin) in His sight. The reason is sin.

Have you ever lied, lusted, hated someone, stolen anything, or taken God's name in vain, even once? These are all sins.

Are you willing to admit to God that you are a sinner? If so, then tell Him right now you have sinned. You can say the words in your heart or aloud—it doesn't matter which—but be honest with God. Now check the box if you have just admitted you are a sinner.

☐ God, I admit I am a sinner in Your eyes.

Spiritual Death

Eternal Life

Now, let's look at the second essential spiritual truth.

Essential Spiritual Truth

#2

The Bible teaches that you cannot save yourself or earn your way to heaven.

Man's sin is a very serious problem in the eyes of God. Your sin separates you from God, both now and for all eternity—unless you are born again.

For the wages of sin is death.
(Romans 6:23)

And you He made alive, who were dead in trespasses and sins.
(Ephesians 2:1)

Wages are a payment a person earns by what he or she has done. Your sin has earned you the wages of death, which means separation from God. If you die never having been born again, you will be separated from God after death.

You cannot save yourself or purchase your entrance into heaven. The Bible says that man is **not redeemed with corruptible things, like silver or gold** (1 Peter 1:18). If you owned all the money in the world, you still could not buy your entrance into heaven. Neither can you buy your way into heaven with good works.

> *For by grace you have been saved through faith, and that not of yourselves; it is the gift of God, not of works, lest anyone should boast.* (Ephesians 2:8–9)

The Bible says salvation is **not of yourselves**. It is **not of works, lest anyone should boast**. Salvation from eternal judgment cannot be earned by doing good works; it is a gift of God. There is nothing you can do to purchase your way into heaven because you are already unrighteous in God's eyes.

If you understand you cannot save yourself, then tell God right now that you are a sinner, separated from Him, and you cannot save yourself. Check the box below if you have just done that.

☐ God, I admit that I am separated from You because of my sin. I realize that I cannot save myself.

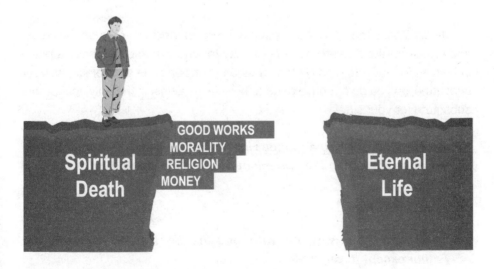

Now, let's look at the third essential spiritual truth.

Essential Spiritual Truth

#3

The Bible teaches that Jesus Christ died on the cross to pay the complete penalty for your sin and to purchase a place in heaven for you.

Jesus Christ, the sinless Son of God, lived a perfect life, died on the cross, and rose from the dead to pay the penalty for your sin and purchase a place in heaven for you. He died on the cross on your behalf, in your place, as your substitute, so you do not have to go to hell. Jesus Christ is the only acceptable substitute for your sin.

For He [God, the Father] made Him [Jesus] who knew [committed] no sin to be sin for us, that we might become the righteousness of God in Him.
(2 Corinthians 5:21)

I [Jesus] am the way, the truth, and the life. No one comes to the Father except through Me.
(John 14:6)

Nor is there salvation in any other, for there is no other name under heaven given among men by which we must be saved.
(Acts 4:12)

Jesus Christ is your only hope and means of salvation. Because you are a sinner, you cannot pay for your sins, but Jesus paid the penalty for your sins by dying on the cross in your place. Friend, there is salvation in no one else—not angels, not some religious leader, not even your religious good works. No religious act such as baptism, confirmation, or joining a church can save you. There is no other way, no other name that can save you. Only Jesus Christ can save you. You must be saved by accepting Jesus Christ's substitutionary sacrifice for your sins, or you will be lost forever.

Do you see clearly that Jesus Christ is the only way to God in heaven? If you understand this truth, tell God that you understand, and check the box below.

❏ God, I understand that Jesus Christ died to pay the penalty for my sin. I understand that His death on the cross was the only acceptable sacrifice for my sin.

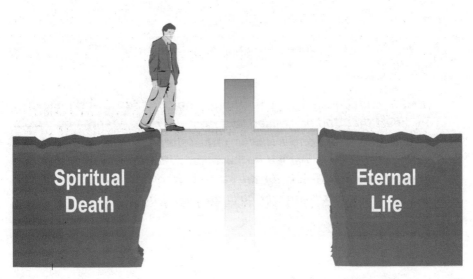

Spiritual Death

Eternal Life

Essential Spiritual Truth

#4

By faith, you must trust in Jesus Christ alone for eternal life and call upon Him to be your Savior and Lord.

Many religious people admit they have sinned. They believe Jesus Christ died for the sins of the world, but they are not saved. Why? Thousands of moral, religious people have never completely placed their faith in Jesus Christ *alone* for eternal life. They think they must believe in Jesus Christ as a real person and do good works to earn their way to heaven. They are not trusting Jesus Christ *alone*. To be saved, you must trust in Jesus Christ *alone* for eternal life. Look what the Bible teaches about trusting Jesus Christ alone for salvation.

Believe on the Lord Jesus Christ, and you will be saved.
(Acts 16:31)

...that if you confess with your mouth the Lord Jesus and believe in your heart that God has raised Him from the dead, you will be saved. For with the heart one believes unto righteousness, and with the mouth confession is made unto salvation.... For there is no distinction between Jew and Greek, for the same Lord over all is rich to all who call upon Him. For "whoever calls on the name of the Lord shall be saved.
(Romans 10:9–10, 12–13)

Do you see what God is saying? To be saved or born again, you must trust Jesus Christ *alone* for eternal life. Jesus Christ paid for your complete salvation. Jesus said, **It is finished!** (John 19:30). Jesus paid for your salvation completely when He shed His blood on the cross for your sin.

If you believe that God resurrected Jesus Christ (proving God's acceptance of Jesus as a worthy sacrifice for man's sin) and you are willing to confess Jesus Christ as your Savior and Lord (master of your life), you will be saved.

Friend, right now God is offering you the greatest gift in the world. God wants to give you the *gift* of eternal life, the *gift* of His complete forgiveness for all your sins, and the *gift* of His unconditional acceptance into heaven when you die. Will you accept His free gift now, right where you are?

Are you unsure how to receive the gift of eternal life? Let me help you. Do you remember that I said you needed to understand and accept four essential spiritual truths? First, you admitted you are a sinner. Second, you admitted you were separated from God because of your sin and you could not save yourself. Third, you realized that Jesus Christ is the only way to heaven—no other name can save you.

Now, you must trust that Jesus Christ died once and for all to save your lost soul. Just take God at His word—He will not lie to you! This is the kind of simple faith you need to be saved. If you would like to be saved right now, right where you are, offer this prayer of simple faith to God. Remember, the words must come from your heart.

God, I am a sinner and deserve to go to hell. Thank You, Jesus, for dying on the cross for me and for purchasing a place in heaven for me. I believe You are the Son of God and You are able to save me right now. Please forgive me for my sin and take me to heaven when I die. I invite You into my life as Savior and Lord, and I trust You alone for eternal life. Thank You for giving me the gift of eternal life. Amen.

If, in the best way you know how, you trusted Jesus Christ alone to save you, then God just saved you. He said in His Holy Word, ***But as many as received Him, to them He gave the right to become the children of God*** (John 1:12). It's that simple. God just gave you the gift of eternal life by faith. You have just been born again, according to the Bible.

You will not come into eternal judgment, and you will not perish in the lake of fire—you are saved forever! Read this verse carefully and let it sink into your heart.

> *Most assuredly, I say to you, he who hears My word and believes in Him who sent Me has everlasting life, and shall not come into judgment, but has passed from death into life.*
> (John 5:24)

Now, let me ask you a few more questions.

According to God's holy Word (John 5:24), not your feelings, what kind of life did God just give you? _____

What two words did God say at the beginning of the verse to assure you that He is not lying to you? _____ _____

Are you going to come into eternal judgment? ☐ YES ☐ NO

Have you passed from spiritual death into life? ☐ YES ☐ NO

Friend, you've just been born again. You just became a child of God.

To help you grow in your new Christian life, we would like to send you some Bible study materials. To receive these helpful materials free of charge, e-mail your request to **info@LamplightersUSA.org.**

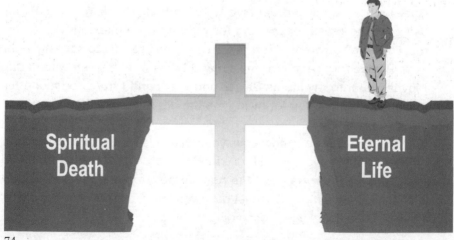

Spiritual
Death

Eternal
Life

APPENDIX

LEVEL 1 (BASIC TRAINING)
STUDENT WORKBOOK

To begin, familiarize yourself with the Lamplighters' *Leadership Training and Development Process* (see graphic on page 76). Notice there are two circles: a smaller, inner circle and a larger, outer circle. The inner circle shows the sequence of weekly meetings beginning with an Open House, followed by an 8–14 week study, and concluding with a clear presentation of the gospel (Final Exam). The outer circle shows the sequence of the Intentional Discipleship training process (Leading Studies, Training Leaders, Multiplying Groups). As participants are transformed by God's Word, they're invited into a discipleship training process that equips them in every aspect of the intentional disciple-making ministry.

The Level 1 training (Basic Training) is *free*, and the training focuses on two key aspects of the training: 1) how to prepare a life-changing Bible study (ST-A-R-T) and 2) how to lead a life-changing Bible study (10 commandments). The training takes approximately 60 minutes to complete, and you complete it as an individual or collectively as a small group (preferred method) by inserting an extra week between the Final Exam and the Open House.

To begin your training, go to www.LamplightersUSA.org to register yourself or your group. A Lamplighters' Certified Trainer will guide you through the entire Level 1 training process. After you have completed the training, you can review as many times as you like.

When you have completed the Level 1 training, please consider completing the Level 2 (Advanced) training. Level 2 training will equip you to reach more people for Christ by learning how to train new leaders and by showing you how to multiply groups. You can register for additional training at www.LamplightersUSA.org.

Intentional Discipleship
Training & Development Process

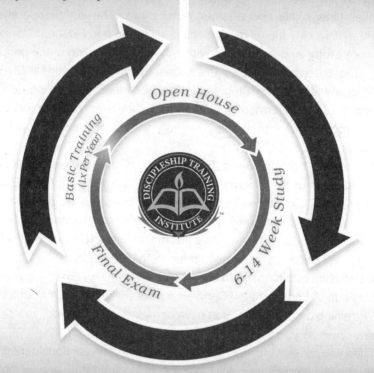

3. Multiplying Groups

The "5 Steps" for Starting New Groups
The Audio Training Library (ATL)
The Importance of the Open House

1. Leading Studies

ST-A-R-T
10 Commandments
Solving All Group Problems

Open House

Basic Training
(1x Per Year)

6-14 Week Study

Final Exam

2. Training Leaders

Four-fold ministry of a leader
The Three Diagnostic Questions

The 2P's for recruiting new leaders
The three stages of leadership training

How to Prepare a
Life-Changing Bible Study
ST-A-R-T

Step 1: _____ and _____.

 Pray specifically for the group members and yourself as you study God's
 Word. Ask God (_____) to give each group member
 a rich time of personal Bible study, and thank (_____) God for
 giving you a desire to invest in the spiritual advancement of each other.

Step 2: _____ the _____.

 Answer the questions in the weekly lessons without looking at the

 _____ _____.

Step 3: _____and _____.

 Review the Leader's Guide, and _____ every truth you missed when
 you originally did your lesson. Record the answers you missed with a
 _____ _____ so you'll know what you missed.

Step 4: _____ _____.

 Calculate the specific amount of time _____ _____ to
 spend on each question and write the start time next to each one in the
 _____ using a _____.

How to Lead a Life-Changing Bible Study

10 COMMANDMENTS

1	2	3
4	5	6
7	8	9
	10	

Lamplighters' 10 Commandments are proven small group leadership principles that have been used successfully to train hundreds of believers to lead life-changing, intentional discipleship Bible studies.

Essential Principles for Leading Intentional Discipleship Bible Studies

1. The 1st Commandment: The _____ Rule.
   The Leader-Trainer should be in the room _____ minutes before the class begins.

2. The 2nd Commandment: The _____-_____ Rule.
   Train the group that it is okay to _____, but they should never be
   _____.

3. The 3rd Commandment: The _____ Rule.
   _____, _____, _____ ask for
   _____ to _____ the _____, _____, and _____
   the questions. The Leader-Trainer, however, should always _____ the
   questions to control the _____ of the study.

4. The 4th Commandment: The ____:____ Rule.
   _____ the Bible study on time and _____ the study on time
   _____ _____. No exceptions!

5. The 5th Commandment: The _____ Rule.
   Train the group participants to _____ on God's Word for answers
   to life's questions.

1	2	3
4 **59:59**	5	6
7	8	9
	10	

6. The 6th Commandment: The _____ Rule.
   Deliberately and progressively _____ _____ participants into the
   group discussion over a period of time.

7. The 7th Commandment: The _____ _____ Rule.
   _____ the participants to get _____ the answers to the
   questions, not just _____ or _____ ones.

8. The 8th Commandment: The _____ Rule.
   _____ the group discussion so you _____ the
   lesson _____ _____ and give each question _____
   _____.

9. The 9th Commandment: The _____-_____ Rule.
   Don't let the group members talk about _____
   _____, _____ _____, or
   _____ _____.

10. The 10th Commandment: The _____ Rule.
    _____ God to change lives, including _____.

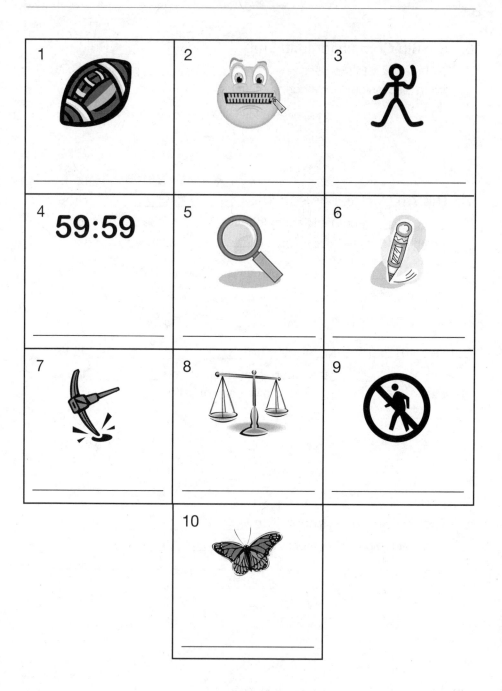

Choose your next study from any of the following titles:

- Joshua 1-9
- Joshua 10-24
- Judges 1-10
- Judges 11-21
- Ruth/Esther
- Jonah/Habakkuk
- Nehemiah
- Proverbs 1-9
- Proverbs 10-31
- Ecclesiastes
- John 1-11
- John 12-21
- Acts 1-12
- Acts 13-28

- Romans 1-8
- Romans 9-16
- Galatians
- Ephesians
- Philippians
- Colossians
- 1 & 2 Thessalonians
- 1 Timothy
- 2 Timothy
- Titus/Philemon
- Hebrews
- James
- 1 Peter
- 2 Peter/Jude

Additional Bible studies and sample lessons are available online.

For audio introductions on all Bible studies, visit us online at www.Lamplightersusa.org.

Looking to begin a new group?
The Lamplighters Starter Kit includes:

- 8 James Bible Study Guides
  (students purchase their own books)
- 25 Welcome Booklets
- 25 Table Tents
- 25 Bible Book Locator Bookmarks
- 50 Final Exam Tracts
- 50 Invitation Cards

For a current listing of live and online discipleship training
events, or to register for discipleship training, go to
www.LamplightersUSA.org/training.

Become a Certified
Disciple-Maker

Training Courses Available:

- Leader-Trainer
- Discipleship Coach
- Discipleship Director

Contact the Discipleship Training Institute
for more information (800-507-9516).

The Discipleship Training Institute is a ministry of
Lamplighters International.